FINAL QUESTIONS

Sola Scriptura

Grand Haven, Michigan

Written and edited by the staff of The Sign Ministries
Designed and illustrated by Scott Holmgren

Published by Sola Scriptura
P.O. Box 770, Grand Haven, MI 49417

Printed in the United States of America

CONTENTS

INTRODUCTION

The study of end-time events, called *Eschatology*, is the biblical study of the last days and the Second Coming of Jesus Christ. The people of God eagerly look for *the blessed hope and the appearing of the glory of our great God and Savior, Christ Jesus,*[1] but when it comes to the timing, nature, and understanding of the events leading up to His return, there is considerable disagreement among believers. Differing interpretations of prophetic Scripture, some based more on man's opinions than actual scriptural teaching, have led to conflicting views about *how* and *when* this period of time will happen. Because these views are controversial, end-time events are widely misunderstood by many believers.

This is not what Christ intended. God inspired the authors of Scripture to *write nothing else to you than what you read and understand*[2] in order that every believer might comprehend the meaning of His message. Sometimes, when reading passages on prophecy, our study habits may actually distort the original intended meaning. We may spiritualize, allegorize, or build a conviction based on one passage without looking at others that deal with the same subject. However, when we read God's Word at face value and compare Scripture with Scripture, the Bible is amazingly clear about the order of end-time events. *The sum of Thy word is truth.*[3]

It is vitally important that we understand God's Word regarding end time events. When Christ addressed the disciples' questions about the end of the age on the Mount of Olives in Matthew 24, He instructed them *see to it that no one misleads you.*[4] Other New Testament writers give us the same warning. At Christ's ascension, He told His disciples to teach and observe *all that I commanded you.*[5]

We can be sure that end-times prophecies will be faithfully and completely fulfilled by God, just like the prophecies concerning Christ's first coming. All the Old Testament prophecies concerning Christ's first coming were literally fulfilled in every detail! It only makes sense to expect that God will be just as precise about fulfilling the prophecies concerning Christ's Second Coming, for God has said *"Truly I have spoken; truly I will bring it to pass. I have planned it, surely I will do it."*[6]

1

WHAT IS THE SEVENTIETH WEEK OF DANIEL?

Daniel's Seventieth Week refers to a seven-year period that will occur at the very end of the age we now live in. What happens during these final seven years is described in many passages throughout the Bible, but particularly in the books of Daniel, Revelation, and in the Gospels. Daniel's Seventieth Week is foundational to the understanding of the timing and sequence of end-time events.

First, it's important to understand that all events of history revolve in some way around the people and land of Israel. The prophet Daniel tells us that *seventy weeks have been decreed for your people.*[1] The Hebrew word for "weeks" literally means "a unit of seven." In context, this seventy week prophecy refers to seventy periods of seven years, or a total of 490 years. Sixty-nine of these "weeks" of years occurred between the order to rebuild Jerusalem in 445 BC and the arrival of Christ in the city on Palm Sunday (a total of 483 years). During the final seven-year period, Israel will be under the domination of an empire controlled by Satan, because when Jesus Christ *came to His own* (the Jews),*... those who were His own did not receive*

Him.[2] In other words, Israel rejected her true Messiah and King, Jesus Christ, at His first coming. So God determined that there would be a period of time between the first sixty-nine weeks and the seventieth week that would bring the opportunity for salvation to the Gentiles (non-Jews). This fulfills God's promise to Abraham, that *in you all the families of the earth shall be blessed.*[3]

Since Israel regained control of her land in 1948, and of Jerusalem in 1967, the events that begin the seventieth week could happen any time. In this final period, Satan will make a last great effort to preserve his control over the earth. Daniel tells us that his empire will be *dreadful and terrifying and extremely strong.*[4] World-wide troubles will begin mildly and increase in intensity as the week (7 years) progresses. Christ told His disciples that *there will be a great tribulation, such as has not occurred since the beginning of the world until now, nor ever shall.*[5]

2

WILL THERE BE AN ANTICHRIST?

Yes, there will be a literal person who will rule the empire of Satan during the Seventieth Week of Daniel. This *man of lawlessness*[1] will be empowered by Satan himself, who will give *his authority to the beast* (Antichrist).[2] The power of his empire will extend *over every tribe and people and tongue and nation.*[3]

The Antichrist, who will *set up the abomination of desolation,*[4] will come from somewhere *out of the north,*[5] possibly Russia or northern Europe. As part of his campaign, Antichrist will *make a firm covenant with the many* (Israel) *for one week.*[6] This *one week* period is the Seventieth Week of Daniel, initiated by the signing of Antichrist's covenant with Israel.

After the signing of the covenant, the world will begin to endure *wars and rumors of wars,*[7] and *in various places there will be famines and earthquakes.*[8] The unsaved world will not recognize the true intentions of this leader. Then at

the midpoint of the week, exactly three-and-a-half years after the signing of the covenant, Antichrist will enter the rebuilt, holy temple of God in Jerusalem, where he will stand *in the holy place*[9] and *will exalt and magnify himself above every god, and will speak monstrous things against the God of gods.*[10] He will demand the worship of all people, and that everyone receive his mark. *No one should be able to buy or to sell, except the one who has the mark.*[11] Antichrist will be given authority *to make war with the saints and to overcome them.*[12]

3

WHAT ARE THE SEVEN SEALS?

In the book of Revelation the apostle John sees *in the right hand of Him who sat on the throne a book written inside and on the back, sealed up with seven seals.*[1] An angel asks, *"Who is worthy to open the book and to break its seals?"*[2] The answer is: *Behold, the Lion that is from the tribe of Judah, the Root of David, has overcome so as to open the book and its seven seals.*[3] Only Jesus Christ, the Lion of Judah, is worthy to open the seals, because He is the only one *without blemish.*[4] The seals are not judgment from Christ, but conditions that have to be met before the punishment of the wicked begins.

The first three seals are three major events that will happen during the first half of the Seventieth Week of Daniel. Christ calls them *the beginning of birth pangs.*[5] The last four seals are major events that will happen during the second half of the week.

The first seal is a multiplying of false christs and false prophets. Jesus said of these false christs, *"See to it that you be not misled."*[6] When the second seal is broken, wars will begin to increase on the earth. The third seal Christ defines by saying, *"In various places there will be famines."*[7]

As the second half of the week begins, the fourth seal will be opened during the beginning of the great tribulation, when Antichrist will begin his relentless pursuit to kill those who oppose him. The fifth seal represents the martyrdom of the saints who refuse to worship Antichrist.

The sixth seal is the sign of the end of the age. It will be a cataclysmic change in the sun, moon, and stars. When talking about this event, the book of Revelation says that *the sun became black as sackcloth made of hair, and the whole moon became like blood; and the stars of the sky fell to the earth.*[8] This will be a terrifying sign for the wicked, because they will know that God is coming to judge them. But it will be a wonderful sign for believers, because they will know that Christ is right at the door to rescue His saints! And with the breaking of the seventh seal the book is opened. Now God's supernatural fiery wrath will be unleashed upon the wicked. *As it happened in the days of Noah,*[9] God's wrath will begin on the same day that Christ rescues the righteous from Antichrist's persecution.

4

WHAT IS THE GREAT TRIBULATION?

The great tribulation will be the time of intense persecution by Antichrist against the nation of Israel and the church of God, those who *hold to the testimony of Jesus.*[1] It will begin at the midpoint of the Seventieth Week of Daniel, when Antichrist *exalts himself above every so-called god or object of worship, so that he takes his seat in the temple of God.*[2]

The great tribulation is not the wrath of God, but the wrath of Satan. Revelation tells us that *the devil has come down to you, having great wrath, knowing that he has only a short time.*[3] Satan will empower Antichrist to lead an effort to eliminate God's faithful people from the face of the earth. *The dragon* (Satan) *was enraged with the woman* (Israel), *and went off to make war with the rest of her offspring* (the church).[4]

Because of the severity of this time, Christ told His disciples that *most people's love will grow cold,*[5] and that many *will fall away and will deliver up one another and hate one another.*[6] God will permit this intense time of testing because the church of the last days will have lapsed into severe spiritual compromise. This testing will *refine* and *purge*[7] the nation of Israel, and separate the *wheat* (real Christians) from the *tares*[8] (look-alike Christians). In this way, God will *purify for Himself a people for His own possession.*[9] Genuine believers will not bow down to Antichrist's demands. To encourage believers during this time, Christ says to *not fear those who kill the body, but are unable to kill the soul.*[10]

5

WHAT IS THE RAPTURE?

Scripture teaches that *God has not destined us for wrath, but for obtaining salvation* (deliverance) *through our Lord Jesus Christ.*[1] In other words, God will remove, or rapture, His people from the earth before His wrath comes. The Rapture is spoken of in Scripture as the gathering together, or deliverance, of the true church to Christ in the clouds at His Second Coming.

Christ taught believers to *be on the alert, for you do not know which day your Lord is coming.*[2] Even though we do not know the exact day and hour, Christ did give us the sequence of events. We know from His teaching and other Scripture that the Rapture will occur *immediately after the tribulation of those days,*[3] after the sixth seal (the sign in the sun, moon, and stars), sometime during the second half of the Seventieth Week of Daniel. The Rapture will happen in the midst of the days when Antichrist is seeking to destroy the believers. Christ said of those days of persecution that *unless those days had been cut short, no life would have been saved. But for the sake of the elect those days shall be cut short.*[4]

The Lord's coming will not be a secret, silent event. The book of 1 Thessalonians tells us that *the Lord Himself will descend from heaven with a shout, with the voice of the archangel, and with the trumpet of God.*[5] In Revelation it says that the sign in the sun, moon, and stars, which will

appear just before the Rapture, will be accompanied by *a great earthquake... and every mountain and island were moved out of their places.*[6] Christ tells us that *just as the lightning comes from the east, and flashes even to the west, so shall the coming of the Son of Man be.*[7] He even says that this sign will be seen by *all the tribes of the earth.*[8] Finally, Christ will *send forth His angels with a great trumpet and they will gather together His elect from the four winds, from one end of the sky to the other.*[9] At His coming, Christ will visibly and abruptly "cut short" the persecution by Antichrist by removing the object of Satan's wrath (believers).

6

WHAT IS THE DAY OF THE LORD?

The awesome Day of the Lord is the climactic event in history when God will pour out His wrath in judgment on *those who do not obey the gospel of our Lord Jesus.*[1] It will begin suddenly and unexpectedly, right after the sign in the sun, moon, and stars, as Christ comes on the clouds to gather His saints. Christ tells us that the Rapture and the beginning of God's wrath will happen on the same day, *as it happened in the days of Noah,*[2] *as happened in the days of Lot.*[3] From that point, Antichrist and Satan will be rendered powerless.

The writers of Scripture associate the Day of the Lord with fire. Zephaniah declares that *all the earth will be*

devoured in the fire of His jealousy, for He will make a complete end, indeed a terrifying one, of all the inhabitants of the earth.[4] Isaiah, Joel, and Peter all make similar statements about the fiery judgment to come.

The Scriptures tell us that those who will be destroyed by God's wrath *did not repent of the works of their hands, so as not to worship demons, and the idols... and they did not repent of their murders nor of their sorceries nor of their immorality nor of their thefts.*[5] So the wrath of God will be a consequence of willful rebellion against a holy God. It will include seven trumpet judgments and seven bowl judgments, ending at the final battle of Armageddon. The trumpet and bowl judgments will destroy the earth, rivers, lakes, and seas. Mankind will be tormented by terrible plagues like skin sores, giant insects, and scorching heat, but they will still not repent.

7

WHEN WILL ISRAEL BE SAVED?

Along with the church, the faithful remnant of Jews will be the target of intense persecution during the second half of Daniel's Seventieth Week. The Jewish remnant will flee to the wilderness where they will be supernaturally protected by God. *And when the dragon* (Satan) *saw that he was thrown down to the earth, he persecuted the woman* (Israel)... *And the two wings of the great eagle were given to the woman, in order that she might fly to the wilderness to her place, where she was nourished for a time and times and half a time* (three and a half years), *from the presence of the serpent.*[1]

After the Seventieth Week is complete, the eyes of the surviving Jews will be opened and *they will call on My name, and I will answer them; I will say "They are My people," and they will say, "The Lord is my God."*[2] Christ their Messiah

will personally lead them from the wilderness where He will then deliver them to a place of protection from the final wrath of God consisting of the seven bowl judgments. They will then be with Him on Mount Zion. At that time all the surviving Jews will be saved. After a forty-five day restoration period, Christ will call the Jews to the restored land of Israel.

8

WHEN DOES GOD TAKE BACK CONTROL OF THE EARTH?

After the completion of the Seventieth Week, the seventh trumpet will be blown, and God Almighty will reclaim divine authority over the earth from Satan. *And the seventh angel sounded; and there arose loud voices in heaven, saying, "The kingdom of the world has become the kingdom of our Lord, and of His Christ; and He will reign forever and ever." And the twenty-four elders... fell on their faces and worshipped God, saying,... "We give Thee thanks, O Lord God,... because Thou hast taken Thy great power and hast begun to reign."*[1]

This event is very significant. Determined in eternity past, it is the culmination of God's cosmic conflict with Satan.

Throughout history, this is the event that Satan has done all in his power to prevent.

When the seventh trumpet is blown, and the rightful rule of earth is restored to God, the remaining followers of Antichrist will still not repent. Revelation tells us *the nations were enraged, and Thy wrath came.*[2] So after the seventh trumpet is blown, the seven bowl judgments will be poured out on the earth, culminating in Armageddon, for the final destruction of the wicked.

9

WHAT IS ARMAGEDDON?

The famous and often misunderstood "Battle of Armageddon" is among the last events of the Day of the Lord; the final confrontation between Christ with His angelic armies of heaven and Antichrist with the ungodly armies of his empire. This will be another effort by Satan to win back his rule of the earth, which he lost at the sounding of the seventh trumpet. This devastating conflict will bring the war between God and Satan to an end.

Revelation says, "*And I saw heaven opened; and behold, a white horse, and He who sat upon it is called Faithful and True;... And the armies which are in heaven, clothed in fine linen, white and clean, were following Him on white horses. And from His mouth comes a sharp sword, so that with it He may smite the nations,... and He treads the wine press of the fierce wrath of God, the Almighty. And on His robe and on His thigh He has a name written, 'KING OF KINGS, AND LORD OF LORDS.'"*[1]

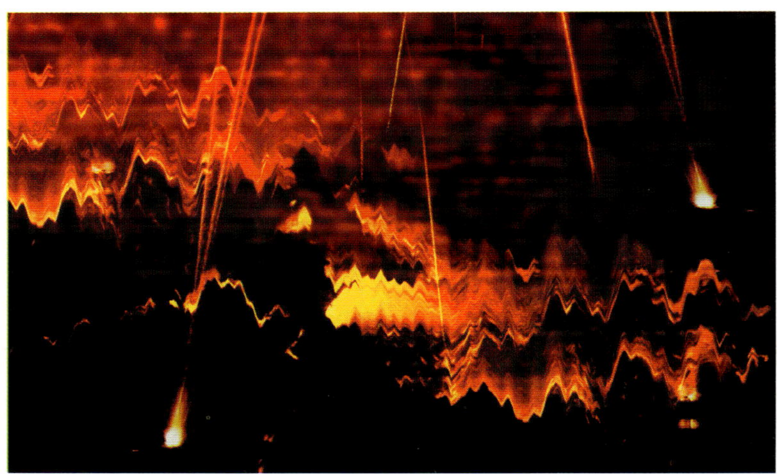

In anticipation of this battle, Antichrist and the false prophet will bring together *the kings of the earth and their armies, assembled to make war against Him who sat upon the horse, and against His army.*[2] They will gather on the plains of Megiddo, about sixty miles north of Jerusalem. Antichrist will be *thrown alive into the lake of fire which burns with brimstone.*[3] The rest of his armies will *be killed with the sword which came from the mouth of Him who sat upon the horse.*[4]

10

WHAT IS THE MILLENNIUM?

The Millennium is the 1000-year period of time when Christ will rule over the kingdom of God on earth. This will be a literal time period that will begin seventy-five days after the end of the Seventieth Week of Daniel.

For glorified saints, the Millennium will fulfill some of the most wonderful promises in the Bible. The Scriptures tell us that there will be *a new heaven and a new earth.*[1] In

addition, the *holy city, new Jerusalem,*[2] where the *river of the water of life* (flows) *clear as crystal,*[3] and where the *tree of life*[4] bears eternal fruit, will descend *down out of heaven from God.*[5]

Glorified saints will inhabit the new Jerusalem as it hovers over the new Mount Zion. This is the glorious holy city which Christ calls *my Father's house* (which has) *many dwelling places*[6] that He has prepared for us. When we as believers reflect on this, we can only bow in worship before our sovereign God. In His kingdom we will enjoy the presence of Christ throughout His glorious reign as King. *They shall be His people, and God Himself shall be among them.*[7] The new earth will be inhabited by saved Israel and the Gentiles who are the sheep of the *sheep* and *goat* judgment.[8]

CONCLUSION

As we have seen, the coming reality of the end of the age will bring with it judgment and wrath for the wicked, but delivery and salvation for believers in Christ. With this in mind, it is very important that each of us consider his eternal condition and present relationship with God.

The Bible tells us that *all have sinned and fall short of the glory of God.*[1] Because of this, our relationship with God has been severed and we all deserve the punishment of hell. But *while we were yet sinners, Christ died for us.*[2] Amazingly, *God so loved the world, that he gave His only begotten Son, that whoever believes in Him should not perish, but have eternal life.*[3] Christ willingly took upon Him the punishment we deserve when He gave His life for us on the cross. By His shed blood, we can have our sins washed away and our relationship with God the Father restored!

But we have to believe. We cannot do anything by ourselves to earn our way into heaven. By acknowledging our sin before the Holy God of all creation, we can have our sins forgiven and be accepted into His kingdom. *That if you confess with your mouth Jesus as Lord, and believe in your heart that God raised Him from the dead, you shall be saved.*[4] What a wonderful God we have, that He would make this provision for us in order to save us! All thanks and praise to Christ Jesus, for now we can go on living our lives for Him and look forward to the blessed hope of His coming!

TIMELINE OF END TIME EVENTS

(numbers refer to questions)

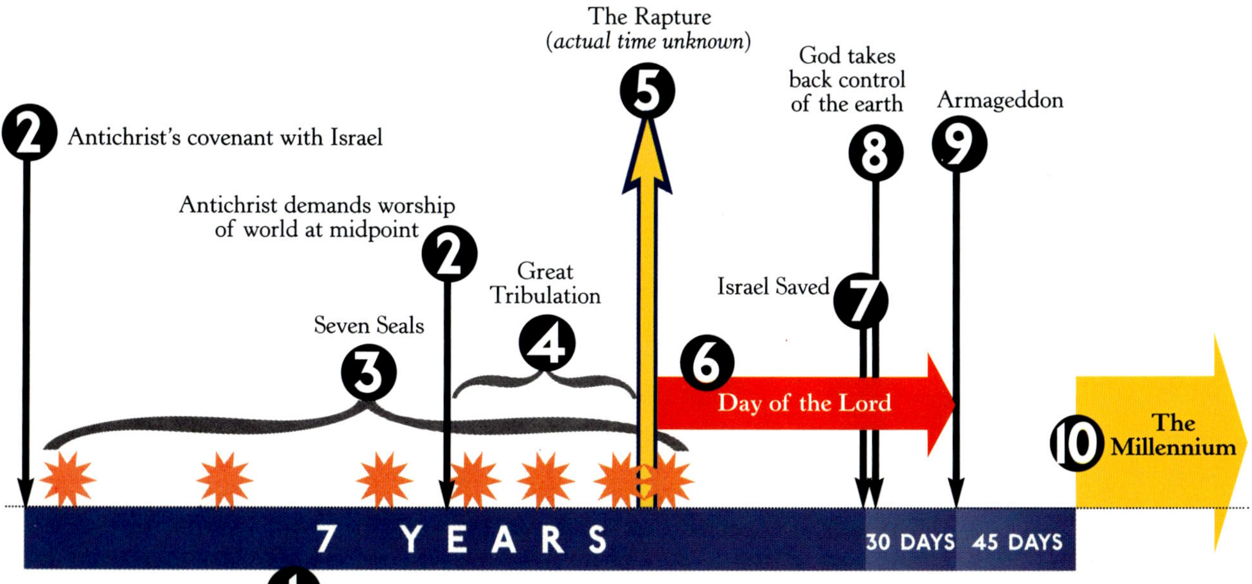

SCRIPTURE QUOTATIONS

INTRODUCTION

1. Titus 2:13
2. 2 Corinthians 1:13
3. Psalm 119:160
4. Matthew 24:4
5. Matthew 28:20
6. Isaiah 46:11

1) WHAT IS THE SEVENTIETH WEEK OF DANIEL?

1. Daniel 9:24
2. John 1:11
3. Genesis 12:3
4. Daniel 7:7
5. Matthew 24:21

2) WILL THERE BE AN ANTICHRIST?

1. 2 Thessalonians 2:3
2. Revelation 13:4
3. Revelation 13:7
4. Daniel 11:31
5. Jeremiah 50:3; Daniel 11:40-41
6. Daniel 9:27
7. Matthew 24:6
8. Matthew 24:7
9. Matthew 24:15
10. Daniel 11:36
11. Revelation 13:17
12. Revelation 13:7

3) WHAT ARE THE SEVEN SEALS?

1. Revelation 5:1
2. Revelation 5:2
3. Revelation 5:5
4. Hebrews 9:14
5. Matthew 24:8
6. Luke 21:8
7. Matthew 24:7
8. Revelation 6:12-13
9. Luke 17:26

4) WHAT IS THE GREAT TRIBULATION?

1. Revelation 12:17
2. 2 Thessalonians 2:4
3. Revelation 12:12
4. Revelation 12:17
5. Matthew 24:12
6. Matthew 24:10
7. Daniel 11:35
8. Matthew 13:30
9. Titus 2:14
10. Matthew 10:28

5) WHAT IS THE RAPTURE?

1. 1 Thessalonians 5:9
2. Matthew 24:42
3. Matthew 24:29
4. Matthew 24:22
5. 1 Thessalonians 4:16
6. Revelation 6:12,14
7. Matthew 24:27
8. Matthew 24:30
9. Matthew 24:31

6) WHAT IS THE DAY OF THE LORD?

1. 2 Thessalonians 1:8
2. Luke 17:26
3. Luke 17:28
4. Zephaniah 1:18
5. Revelation 9:20-21

7) WHEN WILL ISRAEL BE SAVED?

1. Revelation 12:13-14
2. Zechariah 13:9

8) WHEN DOES GOD TAKE BACK CONTROL OF THE EARTH?

1. Revelation 11:15-17
2. Revelation 11:18

9) WHAT IS ARMAGEDDON?
1. Revelation 19:11-16
2. Revelation 19:19
3. Revelation 19:20
4. Revelation 19:21

10) WHAT IS THE MILLENNIUM?
1. Isaiah 65:17; Revelation 21:1
2. Revelation 21:2
3. Revelation 22:1
4. Revelation 22:2,14,19
5. Revelation 21:2
6. John 14:2
7. Revelation 21:3
8. Matthew 25:31-46

CONCLUSION
1. Romans 3:23
2. Romans 5:8
3. John 3:16
4. Romans 10:9

If you have more questions about these issues, or would like more information you may contact us at:

THE SIGN MINISTRIES

call our toll-free number: 1-800-627-5134

or

visit our website: www.signministries.org

or

email us at: info@signministries.org